DOGS

Created by Gallimard Jeunesse
and Pascale de Bourgoing
Illustrated by Henri Galeron

A FIRST DISCOVERY BOOK

SCHOLASTIC INC.
New York   Toronto   London   Auckland   Sydney

Dogs are called
man's best friend.

At the tip
of its muzzle, short
or long, the dog has a
moist snout. This is its nose.

The shape of a
dog's head
depends on its
breed.

A dog's sense of smell is
excellent. It can smell things up to a
million times better than you.

Saint Bernard

Wire Fox Terrier

Have you seen these dogs before?

Great Dane

Dachshund

Chihuahua

Dogs come in all shapes and sizes.

Can you find four large
retrievers and two small
bull terriers?

Dogs have hair called fur...

Short,
  long,
    straight,
    or curly,
  each has its
  own type of fur.

...in all different colors.

A female dog can have four to ten puppies in a litter. She feeds them milk for about two months.

Then
the puppy eats
meat-based foods.
Animals that eat
meat are called
carnivores.

You can understand a dog
by closely watching its actions.

A dog pricks up its
ears to hear better.

It folds back its ears
when it's scared.

It wants you
to pet it.

It would like to
play with you.

A dog goes stiff when it's angry. It curls back its lips
and shows its teeth when it wants to attack.

A dog needs
to sleep a lot.

This one could be dreaming.

But when it is
guarding its house, it often
sleeps with one eye open...

... and might even show
its teeth!

At the slightest whistle,
it comes running …

A dog can find another
animal by following its scent.
It can find its owner this way, too.

A dog often sticks out its tongue,
when it is hot, to cool off.

A dog has strong legs.

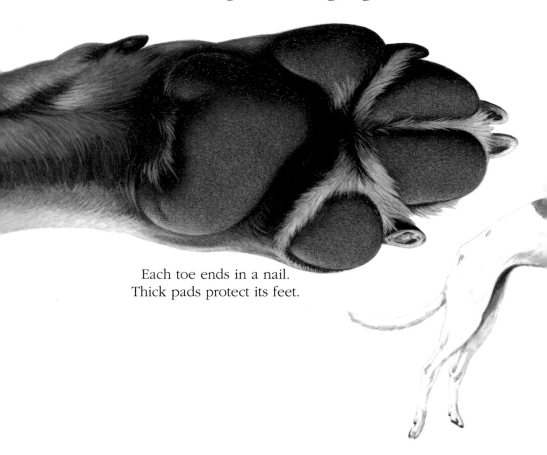

Each toe ends in a nail.
Thick pads protect its feet.

They are muscular and sturdy.

Dogs love to run,
and they can jump very high.

A dog loves
to play…

...and even to swim.

Do you know dogs that
help humans?

A Saint
Bernard
brings help to
people lost in
the mountains.

A dog for the blind guides people who can't see.

Some dogs, like this Border Collie, herd sheep and watch over them.

Sled dogs, like the Siberian Husky and the Alaskan Malamute, gather in a team to pull heavy sleds.

1

2

3

Here are six animals that are related to dogs. Do you know their names?

4

5

6

Titles in the series of
First Discovery Books:

Airplanes
 and Flying Machines
All About Time
Bears
Bees
Birds
Boats
Butterflies
The Camera
Cars and Trucks
 and Other Vehicles
Castles
Cats
Colors
Construction
Dinosaurs
Dogs
The Earth and Sky
The Egg
Endangered Animals
Fish

Farm Animals
Flowers
Frogs
Fruit
Horses
Houses
The Human Body
The Ladybug and
 Other Insects
Light
Monkeys and Apes
Musical Instruments
Night Creatures
Native Americans
Penguins
Pyramids
The Rain Forest
The River
The Seashore
Sports
Trains
The Tree
Turtles and Snails
Under the Ground

Universe
Vegetables in the
 Garden
Water
Weather
Whales

Titles in the series of
First Discovery
Art Books:

Animals
Landscapes
Paintings
Portraits

Titles in the series of
First Discovery
Atlas Books:

Atlas of Animals
Atlas of Countries
Atlas of the Earth
Atlas of People
Atlas of Plants

Library of Congress Cataloging-in-Publication Data available.

Originally published in France in 1990 under the title *Le chien* by Editions Gallimard.

ISBN 0-590-87608-2

Copyright © 1990 by Editions Gallimard.
This edition English translation by Nicole Valaire. Copyright © 1999 by Scholastic Inc.
This edition American text by Mary Varilla. Copyright © 1999 by Scholastic Inc.
This edition Expert Reader: Gina DiNardo-Lash, American Kennel Club.

12 11 10 9 8 7 6 5 4 3 2 1   9/9 0/0 01 02 03 04

Printed in Italy by Editoriale Libraria
First Scholastic printing, March 1999